If poems could carry messages to the dead, Ojanen has crafted the vehicle.
If poems can shatter tired perceptions and reawaken the spirit, these are the poems.
If you lack bright wonder and sorrow dulls your heart, this collection will bring new life.
Roughly for the North is akin to seeing even the oldest dreams anew.

—Debra Magpie Earling. University of Montana, director of creative writing

Some poets celebrate beautiful things. Some poets warn us what we are losing. Some poets remember what we have lost, and in remembering hold onto still. These poems do this and more. Ojanen teaches you how to stay alive. These poems look unflinchingly at the daily, the romantic and the unromantic, the pink flesh of salmon, the river-blue veins on her aaka's hands, and "the yellow guts of crab wrenched out of them by the orange rubber-gloved hands" relegated to commercial seafood plants. Saints, ghosts, loved ones, and angels dwell in it all. The caribou persist, the birds return. It is what is and what will be, as it has always been.

Ojanen's vision is keen and piercing, and the weight is a welcome grounding, like roots. And from it, we grow.

These are poems one wears out into the world. They are poems to dwell in.

—Abigail Chabitnoy Kerstetter. Author of *How to Dress a Fish*

Roughly for the North is a book of love, homage, and redemption. Ojanen's love for her aaka (grandmother) opens her imagination to deep memory, dreams, and spirits. In this evocative and moving sequence of poems she pays homage to her family, her Inupiaq ancestors, and the land and sea that offered and goes on offering sustenance for their lives. She also sketches the sad backstory of Ugiuvak, Alaska (King Island), her grandparents' home, until the Bureau of Indian Affairs closed the school and forced the children to go to school on the mainland. As a result, by 1970 all the island people had moved or been relocated to the mainland, effectively ending their traditional way of life.

Ojanen's beautiful book addresses her grandmother's spirit, and yet those of us who read this book will be privileged to listen as "even now the residual tenderness / travels across the sterile page," and she sings a strong and memorable redemption song.

—Greg Pape. Author of *Four Swans* and *American Flamingo*

I have looked forward to this beautiful book for a long time. Carrie Ojanen's poems light up a place so few of us know; they see through the opacities of hard climates, long dark days, and rigorous means of survival. Ojanen illuminates her homeland with the powers of international forms and wide-ranging languages. She reveals her Inupiat northland to the lower countries. This is a very smart book about love for family and place, and about Ojanen's determination to preserve what remains.

—Daniel Lamberton. Author of *On the River through the Valley of Fire*, and director of the humanities program at Walla Walla University

T0164456

ROUGHLY FOR THE NORTH

BY CARRIE AYAĠADUK OJANEN

Text © 2018 University of Alaska Press

Published by
University of Alaska Press
P.O. Box 756240
Fairbanks, AK 99775-6240

Cover design by UA Press.
Interior design by 590 Design, fiveninetydesign.com

Cover image is a line drawing by Tikasuk Cassandra Johnson of Cecilia Awałuq Muktoyuk
dancing. The drawing is based on a photograph by Peggy Fagerstrom (on page viii), taken at the
fiftieth wedding anniversary celebration for Cecilia and Edward Muktoyuk Sr.

Back cover image of King Island by Carrie Ojanen.
Detail image of *uġiłhaaq* by Andrew Cockerham.

Library of Congress Cataloging in Publication Data

Names: Ojanen, Carrie Ayaġaduk, author.
Title: Roughly for the North / by Carrie Ayaġaduk Ojanen.
Description: Fairbanks, AK : University of Alaska Press, 2018. |
Identifiers: LCCN 2017059966 (print) | LCCN 2018001977 (ebook) | ISBN
    9781602233638 (ebook) | ISBN 9781602233621 (pbk. : acid-free paper)
Classification: LCC PS3615.J36 (ebook) | LCC PS3615.J36 A6 2018 (print) |
    DDC 811/.6dc23
LC record available at https://lccn.loc.gov/201705996

for Cecilia Awetuq Muktoyuk

CONTENTS

≋

PART THREE: EPILOGUE

ACKNOWLEDGMENTS

Iliġanamiik, with heartfelt thanks, to the journals in which my poems have previously appeared.

Prairie Schooner: "Blue Cabin" and "All Her Breath Is Gone"

Louisville Review: "Aaka," as "Auka,"

As/Us Journal: "Someday this may apply to you too, so pay attention." and "Fifth Saint, Sixth & Seventh"

Illġanamin, Joan Naviyuk Kane, for publishing "Afterlife, III," "Motion," "Swim Across" (which is part of the longer poem "Aqpik"), "Roughly for the North" (which appeared in the essay "Awałuq"), and "Caribou" in *Yellow Medicine Review.*

Illġanamin, Andrew Cockerham, for your endless support and love, you have my heart. Illġanamik Mom and Dad. To Dan Lamberton, Linda Andrews, Jillany Wellman, Nari Kirk, Johannes Falkenthall, July Oskar Cole, John Myers, Maren Vespia, Molly Curtis, Greg Pape, Prageeta Sharma, Angelica Lawson, Brian Blanchfield, Debra Earling, and to countless others who have helped me along the way, thank you.

BLUE CABIN

PART ONE

BLUE CABIN

The driftwood rack hangs barren,
the fish do not hang in long, low rows
impossible to walk beneath without brushing
orange flesh, translucent as cut glass
and dripping amber oil. The blue cabin is quiet,
the swan wing broom and the sand still

on the linoleum floor.

Inside, flies bounce on the windows
with no one to let them out.
Outdoors, the flies do not buzz
close to the fish rack, their maggot hatchery,
though there is no wind to keep them away from fish,
there are no fish this year.

Aaka, I'm sorry I'm away
at school, while you grow old, trapped
in a small house fifty miles from camp,
in a town without fish racks, sitting beside Aapa
in the kitchen eating last year's fish,
half-dried and boiled.

I should be home, watching you
cut fish, ulu in hand at the cutting table,
stained with black blood and slippery.
I should be trying to cut fish heads off.
The ulu unmanageable in my inexperienced hand
would slide back and forth as I tried to find the place

between the gills and body, to bear down upon
the spine. It's hard to crack it,
and the bloodline bisected would gush over me,
as it did the one day we stood there, my mother,
her sister, you and I. You laughed,
we all laughed as the black blood

slid down my pink windbreaker.
With the ulu I traced the backbone:
horizontal jagged cuts yanked
meat from bones. Ragged and mashed fillets,
laughter and stories from mother of mangled fillets
while you laughed without stories
as you found the place between the gills and the body.
As you broke the spine, the blood did not
flow over you. As you unzipped from white bones
the orange flesh, it landed heavily in your hand.

Aaka, I write the same thing, over and over.

ALL HER BREATH IS GONE

the gnats swarm around my hood
pulled tight around my glasses,
the blueberries begin to droop
on their branches, the rain
drops cause leaves to cling
to my fingers, the red leaves
to my fingers, the red leaves
in the white bucket, some berries
taste sour to my tongue.
the gnats bite my upper lip,
but the water on my hands keeps
them away from the blue veins
and raw red knuckles. how quiet
it is, how still, after the retired men
drive by, hunting from their old blue
trucks.

all her breath is gone
from the curve of the bone
white lichen antlers
to the withered
willow leaves,
but we all cling

to the land and we say our
prayers to the red
salmon, scales breaking
against the net,
please don't take the long drink

on top of that hill,
the gray hill there,
to the left of the park sign,
are rocks pressed down by some
historic weight, now dissipated,
crushed together, like tiles,
herringbone patterned. I want
to say that weight is still felt.

THE SOUL'S SILVER SIDE IS SPECKLED BLACK

scales hinged, fastened, indented into the soul's
skin. a horizontal shadow greens its back.
the soul has pink serrated gills to filter air
the soul sometimes deep at sea

searches—a sharp tail flick—zips hard—
muscles rip electric—gills timpani—silk
heart surges—air bladder expands—then sky

whiplash-body arcs—
                tail water ripples down—

gripped in teeth—body crushed between palette
and sleek blue tongue—an insect—marooned
by wind gust—exoskeleton cracked between
the soul's small, even teeth.

the soul's eye does not blink
                      sees everything
from the moment it hatches—shivers
      into form
                what is remembered from all these things
                what in all that depth most beautiful
                        most sacred

in your unfolding, sacred soul
                when I bear this knife down upon your spine
hear my prayers
                for everyone I love, I love the best I can
                I loved her, bear this message to her if you can.

A A K A ,

hello, beloved, after the dark
has shadowed you, you are still fragile,
fragile in your pajamas as the fall
spreads its cold over the expanse of water
and the crying crane
V their way south.

I have flown south,
beloved, my memories of summer grow dark,
my crane
breast grows fragile
crying over waters,
tears fall.

I fall
from flight in dreams, fall south,
the earth spinning, its waters
blurring dark,
your fragile
face always craning

up at me before you disappear into that crane
form, that graceful form falling,
your fragile
image wavering south
as the sky grows dark,
as the shadows grow across the water.

Across the water,
I see you dance your crane
dance, lift your dark
wings and let them fall,
rise and fall facing me, I am south
and your cry so far, it reaches me so fragile.

The film over the waters, if fragile
is beautiful, a filigree of lace over the waters,
ice etching its way south,
as delicate as the wavering crane
falling
into the dark,
the dark so fragile
this fall, like a ripple on the water,
I crane my face away from the south to seek you.

THE GHOST OF THE BLIND BERRY PICKER

Hey, did you see the geese?
I saw you lying there,
they flew just overhead,
you seemed to stay so still.

The geese flew low, so close
I feared their legs and lice.
So close their bellies brushed
The air-caves of my eyes.

AQPIK

At the Mouth of the Eldorado and Flambeau Rivers

Lagoon rises black with seaweed
and sallowly retracts, wind rises
salt scented, the islanders scream on their rocks
and rise on white wings. Nobody talks,
gazing salmonberries divine an end,
the orange berries musk the air.
Shrunken pumpkin patch, tongue-soft berries
stick to bucket sides. Sky sits on the horizon
and watches cloudberries fall into blue pails.

On the river-far hill, brown backs bend and rise.
Perhaps the blind ghost comes near,
the leaves grow brittle, reindeer
thrash wildly towards water,
thunder and a terrific splash.
Raising looking glass, the far backs transform
into birds, rise up on long wings,
long dances, long necks, long.

Feathered belly only bullet
stops. The dark V flight.
Crane my father killed we kept the feet from,
totems of fright. We watched bird bodies
knowing, smooth against bellies, long legs pressed.
Sand hills leap with some light
leaping arms cannot grasp or feel.

She's flying somewhere,
her thin arms rise, lift and fall
lift and fall into what sky?
One last view, her rock island,

she rises like breath exhaling,
exhaling, and never catch stop.

What skin touching skin in the first
home of her love will she wake to? Her body will settle
into his sleeping shoulder while gulls cry.

I'm so dizzy and then the waking ache,
somewhere a spider crawls, tapioca sack
to a black-star back, long-hair legs
play lichen marrow keys, forward and back.

It will take a long time to find her,
she will wander over tundra picking berries,
she will not notice me but she is all I see
flowered uġiłhaaq sky. Her fingers fumble,
the orange globe slips down to me.

Everything pushes forward but the sea
who sighs, retouches what it left, and leaving
leaves again. The sea belly slides pitted, pimpled, gored,
clatter-scrape rocks through shift and slip,
scoots through motors
rust mangled, toss-entangled
dump heap. The sea sweats
arcane washer machines,
fat men leg-tripped, white
barrel bodies, leg sticks straight,
mosquitoes' net breaks.
Calder mobile coffee spit.

Swim Across

My aaka watches from the cabin
window my cousin's brown body plunge
into the cold. A singing starts. The host of jellyfish,
veined pink, quaver, they will not sting. Our driftwood sticks
swirl their translucent tremblings.
I know Aaka will take us in dripping,
staring, gray-cloud eyes.

She wets thread in her mouth. The light
comes through the window, almond
fingernails and baby-powder scent,
the worn quilt and stained sheet.
She smiles distantly and moves
small-body grace. Beside her, Julie's red
candles rest unburned, Aaka stokes the woodstove.

The tablecloth is rolled in the corner. Worn towels hang
stiffly above the stove. We will rub the water from
our hair and icy drops from our faces. Sand
will crumble from our feet, sand will settle
into linoleum cracks, Aaka will sweep most out the door.

The far bank recedes into muddy
grasses. I step into the water,
minnows shadow dart from out the rocks, the small boat
grates against the shore, the yellow-rope reflection sways,
cousin calls my name, his seal-head bobs,
the water reaches my calf, I turn to look
at the cabin window, and she's gone.

Holy Mother, if I begin to pray—
bow-spray seas salmon-shine, the silent tern sails on,
plankton swarm, broom-sweep baleen,
the slick slick slick paddle.
Barnacles cling molar beautiful,
the white stars sweep blue-whale skin,
Our Lady of the Bering Sea.

Aaka's Catholic radio station drones
sleepily in the sun, her brown fingers
stitch coarse seal skin.

BREAK THE DISHES OVER HER BARROW

Into the old woman's house the cup,
mug, flatware, doodad boxes stacked.
Two lanky sisters I saw with their mother
at the thrift store lounged

on two old loose-jointed for-sale chairs
in front of pots straining full of ladles
wooden chipped metal stirring spoons
straining spoons, whisks, meat forks.

Lank hair swept from their faces, the smaller
shifted slightly, the older straightened up.
We got out and smiled. We walked behind
them to the table of look-past-them mugs,

the girls' owl necks turned their heads
behind their backs to watch us clank
through ceramic bowls—"There's more
in the house," they said. "Oh, is there?"

we replied as we eased past soup pots—
enamel black-and-white spot stainless
aluminum rusted. Inside, their mother
smiled in stacks of purses. Old,

old purses, cracked plastic leather
one-shoed mismatched tennis and aged
dress-leather shoes. A small round table,
formicaed (like our first kitchen table)

and covered in yellow bowls, red bowls, mismatched
rooster bowls, Chinese letter bowls,
blue Danish and Pyrex bowls, stacked high
and precarious. I wanted the yellow bowls

like Aaka's yellow Pyrex mixing bowls, Mom
wanted soup pots for planting kale,
lettuce and Swiss chard, grown beneath
plastic through three-month summer

and month-long fall. Behind the table
an aluminum samovar, in the sink dirty
dishes, on the rack dry. "Are these all for sale?"
I asked. She nodded, "Yep, we've got to sell all
the stuff before we can move in. There's more in the bedroom."
It was so small. The bed looked so small.

Worn walls, window light dusty, the green army
blanket seemed to sum it up. I didn't have
the heart to catalog it all. I stacked

the bowls I garnered, the cooking pot set still in plastic.
I asked the mother, "How much for all this?"
"Make an offer." I looked at Mom, "Twenty-five?"
The woman said, "Sure."

We didn't ask about the old woman. Whether she moved,
whether she died. We drove home and washed the weevils
out of dishes, washed the dust.

What bone broke or what emptiness—
the firewood box, the cupboard, the ash tray in the sink—
what lapse lifted her from the house,
shook out her memory of things and place,
unlinked property and set her down—her hand still
reaching for the stirring spoon, her feet
still sliding into her slippers, her fingers still tracing
the outside rim of the blue bowl—

≋

HAGIOGRAPHY

PART TWO

SIXTH SAINT

You have been meditating in silence a long time, Aapa.
Fingers knotted over the centerline scar
running up your breastbone riveted
on each side by red-knot scars.

I read your memoir.

What you must think of—so long sitting here—
the BIA did not send another teacher to your island,
wrested your school-aged children away
as you stood to get on the boat in Nome. Ugiuvak—home
    without your eldest children—
the movies you made to try to convince them to send another
    teacher
to King Island, to bring your children home.
We watched those movies together in Nome,
your children and grandchildren
a white sheet hung up in the hall
movie projector whirring as you narrated
a home the youngest of us do not know.
The film spotted and marred with seawater
from fierce winter storms.

How we all watched, how we all sat pressed together
and listened. How you smiled and laughed.

Now nearly deaf, you read lips only if they speak Inupiaq.

There is so much I want to ask you with my naluaġmiut tongue.

You took a picture of yourself over sixty years ago—
how young and strong you stood. Shoulders back, leaning
against your harpoon. Standing on the ice,

the crush of the free ice
slammed against the shore ice—a pressure ridge—
behind you. Wearing a fur parka with its white
winter-hunting canvas cover. Your Siberian
seal hook in hand, rope
circling your arm and shoulder.

You taught Uncle Harry how to braid rope
like that. I watched him sit at the work table,
his summer-tanned hands working the nylon
into a seamless loop—for crab pots at the seafood plant.
Your ropes were pulled and dried tendons.

You wrote the last time you killed a seal
with your harpoon two men hunting with you
were later hit by a drunk driver
and killed in Nome. I don't believe anyone
could hit anyone accidentally in Nome.

But you didn't want to write about that.

As I watch, you stir, a beautiful light
glows in your eyes. You smile,
your white eyebrows raise, you start to speak.

*It was Christmas long, long ago, and the People gathered in the
qagri—like the English word clubhouse, there was a men's qagri and
a carving qagri and a communal qagri. Everybody got together then
to celebrate Christmas. The priest and the schoolteachers were wrap-
ping presents for everyone in the schoolhouse. We ate agutaq and we
danced late into the night.*

Aapa, your belly rises with laughter
as old times cast light through your form.

We didn't get much news back then. Before we got the radio in. We waited and heard news only once or twice a year. We didn't hear news all winter until we went by umiaq over to the other villages. Then we'd hear who died and who was born, who got married. We'd get news from the outside world.

FIFTH SAINT, SIXTH & SEVENTH

Gabriel, sing great-grandpa's song,
head thrown back, black hair gleaming
gray at your temples. So handsome, you,
great-uncle—my Ava—I imagine my Aapa
looked like you when he was younger,
deep, dark skin and half-moon smile
gleaming, you laugh the same laugh—huh huh huh huh!

Did your heart break, as his, leaving the island—
he stayed an extra winter, left his eldest children
in Nome for school, lived on Ugiuvak—the place for winter—
   with aaka
and their smallest children—
Mom, age four, was there—and that 16mm
camera recording the last winter
of his traditional life.

Recording that last winter to convince the BIA to send another
   teacher.

The film was ruined by the August storms.
They wouldn't have watched it anyway.
                     Those fuckers.

O God, reading Aapa's accounts ruptures
                   everything forever.

Aapa never sings.
       But sing, Gabriel, sing, sing grandpa's song.

Mom and Aya Margaret will stand up to dance.
We welcome everyone to dance with us.

You all broke, I know, everyone shattered

        Aaka and Aapa and their sad kitchen life,
        eyes graying the straight, dusty streets
        of Nome.

Everybody lost themselves in drink for years.
Some are still lost.

      ≈≈≈≈

Sing, Gabriel, sing.

How beautiful our women are—
wearing floral uġiłhaaqs,
dancing—that passionate precision—
your Frances, Aaka, Marie, Mom, Margaret, Caroline, Marilyn,
and your granddaughters—in a line—motions memorized.

And then, the song is over.
They move back to their seats.

Please, Ava, as we always do,
sing the song again, a second time,
and a second time they will stand up to dance.

≈≈

THIRD SAINT

my lips touch your cheek—
age-curved below high cheekbones,
you are beautiful—your white hair
rising. dear woman, I see how imperial
you are, how fierce. why shouldn't
you be, born Inupiaq and white in 1916,
it just wasn't done. you lived chaffed
between worlds. but you taunt back
through time.

I study you, the left sag of your mouth,
you are talking. your left hand rises
index finger pointing. your hands—
you know your hands, I know, but I must
study them, I must remember them
now, I must speak of them, I must write of them,
why?

your hands are worn. small, like mine,
but yours have touched the warm interiors
of so many animals—each animal speaks
from each crease of your skin—I hear them
their voices rise with your hands. their songs
grow louder as you motion until their songs
fill the room, until their presence
fills the room, and you are calm
in the presence of their voices,
you hear them as you sit, your hands resting
on your stomach, you hear them speaking,
their voices weave the stories
of your husband and your sons and your daughters
and your father and your mother and your grandparents
and their parents, the voices
tie you together, all together.

all those songs, all those voices,
all those souls sing through your body,
making every part of you beautiful and whole.

and you are beautiful and you are whole.

O Catherine.

THE BERRY PICKER II

She has brown hands with rivers deep and blue,
she plucks the salmonberries from their stems,
she moves, bent over, in and out of view.

The misty air is berry musk imbued.
The orange globes blush between her fingertips.
She has brown hands with rivers deep and blue.

I wake, my sweater dusted with dew,
I thought I heard a bucket plunk, I dreamt,
she moved, bent over, in and out of view.

With berries my bucket's laden, my heart with rue.
Each berry pressed and bucketed repeats lament,
she had brown hands with rivers deep and blue.

In sleep I seek her in that other world,
I follow after, I trace her every step—
she moves, bent over, in and out of view.

Am I still dreaming? My waking eyes confused,
sometimes awake I swear I smell her scent.
She has brown hands with rivers deep and blue.
She moves, bent over, in and out of view.

SECOND SAINT

Her hand at that angle suggests the verge
and border. She has the look. She has
the look.
           Examine her silk-screened image,
her image too stolid to shimmer.

flesh is the . . . how do I say it, the glory of

Her image murmurs, I didn't catch it.
Never ask her to repeat anything. Things
are meant to be lost from language,

but images—*how can her T-shirt be that*
purple?
           or that wrinkled.
her teeth,
           yes, they sit sideways
to each other. Get a good look at the ones
in the back, *comme les français au café*
they've had long conversations over cigarettes.

the sweets *qui sont impeccable ce matin*—listen—
they've whole conversations they meant
to at last expel, never meant to leave
in mind. No, she wasn't really French, except
her teeth. Look.
           Her elbow is a whorl,
an eddy, where her skin's deep waters
show their power. The currents lead smooth
into the breakwaters, her knuckles rise like waves,
smooth into the lapping touch, oh, but she
was strong as water.

She was. *See how high*
her curly hair rises, it expels all evil around her.
I know. I have seen it, but do not look, not now.
Not until your gaze moves to her bare feet.

They are cupped by air, just rising above the
tile floor,
         the gray tiles splotched with mica.
Don't mention she is sitting. These things
aren't essential to the order of examination.
Her calluses yellow, thick, her feet like roots
drawing power.

We must note the air beneath her feet
is not shadowed. Where would we find such
shadows in her presence? She was such
a lion such shadows scattered. I close my
eyes, I see her in my mind, I know her
look so well, I trace her legs,
staunchly crossed, her jeans faded,
ankle-frayed. Perhaps not staunchly
crossed. Her belly rises to her breasts,
crests there and slopes naturally to
her shoulders, like mine, wide.

FIRST SAINT

I was three when she died, but I remember her, Aunt Juliana. Looking at the records, it was a rough summer. My aapa's parents died that summer. Mary Muktoyuk, in June. Stanislaus followed her in July. And Julie died, too, in July. Mary was eighty-six, Stanislaus eighty-eight, but Julie was only thirty-one. Her death hit my grandparents hard. Julie was their first natural born child. They thought they couldn't have any children. They adopted their eldest, Aunt Yayuuk, then right after they adopted Yayuuk, Aaka got pregnant with Julie.

I remember Julie before she got sick—she was tall, she had long black hair, black-brown eyes. She was beautiful. In my memory, she is always moving towards me, reaching down to pick me up. I remember her without sound. I can't remember her voice. I can't remember the sound of her step. I remember approaching Aaka's house and she came down the porch steps, walked through mud, and swept me up. She was always smiling.

Julie got sick. I remember asking Mom why. She said it was because Julie didn't take her medicine. As a kid, for a long time, I thought this was true. Then later, I asked Mom what really happened. It was stomach cancer.

In Aaka's living room, there is a couch against one wall and a bed against the other. When we'd go over to visit, Julie would be lying on the bed. There was a green hospital pan on the floor next to her head and she would reach for it and vomit.

I think, as she got sicker, she started to sleep with Aaka and Aapa in their bed. One of my last memories of Julie is being led into Aaka and Aapa's bedroom, Julie was in the bed. She leaned down towards me and handed me a wrapped present. It was a Care Bear. She gave gifts to everyone as she was dying.

When I think about this now, when I think of her giving gifts as she lay dying, when I think of her generosity, I am moved.

Dad and Mark Weaver Sr., a neighbor, built Julie's coffin. I remember running my finger along the dark brown smooth edge of it after they finished building it. It didn't make me sad. I understood she would be placed in it, but I didn't understand she was dead. I tossed dirt into the grave with everyone at the funeral.

Mom says Dad and Julie didn't get along all that well. Julie was very bossy. Mom says Julie, Yayuuk, and Loretta practically raised her and the younger kids. The summer after Julie's death, in June, my sister Carin Juliana was born. Aaka and Aapa gave Carin Julie's Inupiaq name.

My sister, Mom says, is a lot like Julie. She is strong-willed, she is bossy, and everyone feels what she is feeling around her. As a child, when Carin was being particularly bossy, Dad would say, "Julie, Julie," in a voice both loving and astonished. Dad and Carin get along well together.

Whenever Carin enters Aaka and Aapa's house, Aapa looks up, a smile spreads over his entire face, his eyes light up, he catches his breath and says, "Juliana. Juliana." He'll laugh and beam as she walks over to greet him with a kiss. When Aaka was alive, she would smile at her, her eyes glowing. For a while after Carin entered the room, they couldn't take their eyes off of her.

Carin and I struggled as children to get along. Since I am older than her, I think I should be the bossy one. But she is indomitable. When I think of Julie and her generosity, I wish I treated Carin better, I wish I was kinder to her.

Years ago, just six months to a year after Aunt Loretta died, Julie's daughter came to visit. Her name is Nelena. Julie adopted her out to a family who moved to Wasilla. Nelena wanted to meet her extended birth family. She looks so much like Julie, dark crescent eyes and wide smile. She was the sun. Our family orbited around her while she visited us. She looks so much like Julie. Aaka watched her with love and shyness. Aapa laughed with joy every time he saw her. All us cousins wanted to always be hugging her.

FIRST SAINT (WITHOUT SOUND)

dark winter swept Julie's hair
blue—winter lights shaken
frost pollen green-gold
she—always walking
towards—forever reaching

down, her face of joy

> a moon on her forehead, a star on her
> chin

she—the saint of longing
to be near,
      beckons   (and stars. the winter-browned flowers
                     rise from the snow stiffly)

a pink bear
      in hand. our voices rise   Julie, Julie
                      and her image
waves, our breath catches
sail. watch the careful preparations

our hands make—the smooth
corner of the box, the earth clumped
and crumbled, falling broken
from our hands.
      she walks down the stairs   (every motion, motions)

reaching—she walks through mud
and sweeps me up, my nose
              in that sweep of winter
that sweep of night.   but what quick exit.

return with stars, they will fall
from your mouth (without suffering)
we will gather every one, our palms
shining, we will trace your every
move forever in our minds.

REMEMBERING THE ANGELS'
INVISIBLE BODIES

The paired condors' great gray shoulders hunch
on Cape Nome. Their great wings
lifted them
from the skeletal radio towers in Tennessee, they rose. They
    rose

until the atmosphere lilied and the earth and sea stretched light.
They saw lines of light and they felt cold above
the mountains that looked like ashes
they felt wind grip
the forefront
of their wings. The earth spun
while they felt still
and they were
still, but only for a while. It felt like they had gone too far.

As they came down,
the earth
was
barren and the land
was

naked. As they fell back
into the air, there
were white waves on the sea

they circled above
the cliffs that seemed
so small. Then a sound,
and they caught
another sound.

The earth took
form, they saw bushes. They landed in
the summer light, but they did

not know that it was summer.
And it was as if they were invited,
and it was as if they were here

the only ones
of their race, the only ones of their species,
the only
ones
in the universe,
or at least the earth. And seeing
their surroundings, they were
bewildered, but they were quiet, they saw no creator
to demand answer from, and perhaps

he had granted them this new home—
The land was brown and when they lifted their
wings, there was no place that seemed
like home, there was no
place that seemed different
from place. They soared from rock
outcropping to low hill and saw strange

creatures, heard strange sounds. But always
there were people
and they knew they had not reached paradise.
When they stopped searching, they made
rest on Cape Nome. They sat looking
at the sea, and they sat waiting by
the sea, and they sat,
and then came December.

CARIBOU

He said he saw the caribou herd near Teller
in the spring before the cows dropped their calves.
He was driving through some bad weather
and they appeared before him on the gravel
road. They were like ghost ships at sea, plunging
in and out of swells, appearing and
disappearing in the fog. He nudged
his truck forward to look at the band
more closely and their spots became images
on a reel, like flashes of the salmon
in a stream swimming towards him
as he stood knee-deep, their bodies, their fins
grazing him, their bellies thick and swelling,
their fecundity overwhelming his gaze.

MOTION

We're driving to the restaurant
and we're not really awake.
I look at the man in suspenders
and I see America
goes where she always goes
at six a.m., to breakfast
before dawn.

The old men
at breakfast cannot say
it anymore, in their white
work shirts and blue
union hats,
they all want to say it,

The white hairs are shaved from my face
but I won't shower unless you've died.

I listen like it's the scratchy radio
on the way to the lake. On the last
hill that I can hear NPR, Lourdes Garcia-Navarro says
something about jihad.

The rocks polish
their skulls in gravel, the retired hunters
pull farther left, red taillights flicker.

It may be arduous to say after
my throat gets caught on before
and then is falling, I can't stand
this window anymore.

He reads the obituaries,
places appear without time.
The spring chooshes beside me,
the water bottle drips in my hand,
my palm cups fresh blueberries,
this hand holds the shattered red rock
and that one the littered beer can.
The salmon swim in red defensive
circles in the lake shallows, their mates
lie dead on the shore. I see their round eyes,
sometimes their hooked noses, their male bodies
circle and circle.

THE SOUL IS A

salmon

is the sun

series on the sea

a thousand

suns

each upwelling is the soul

again

again

look

how the sea is today—so gentle

she sucks the pebbles

softly

lips round beads loosely

the sun shines the smooth rocks

wetted in her mouth

I will lift each salmon

I will lift them up

I will heft each soul

I will hold it up

chest high

the salmon's scales glint on my fingers   each scale a sun

how beautiful is this salmon, this salmon I hold in my hands

see its body, net-wrenched as it is

perfect

~~~

this is how to unfold flesh—

we eat together, on the floor
the red tablecloth beneath us.
the enamel pans filled full—dense
brown meat, pink flesh,
salmon egg sacks, coffee cans
shine with seal oil, gleam
green with *syrah*, our hands
reach down—the flesh flaking
in our fingers.
     she is smiling
my Aaka, laughing,
her dark eyes gleaming.
     Aġuvitisi.
     Sit down with us.

Syramic. The seal oil is passed, poured out,

her fingers glisten
    how brown her fingers
      how lovely the deep blue veins

SOMEDAY THIS MAY APPLY TO YOU TOO, SO PAY ATTENTION.

These are forgotten words I want to remember
deft knife, the scent of
                              aren't we
lost
          I choose them
                              they're made of
cold sand-blood, we're still
                                        a small animal
a plastic bag, a seal pup. I'm made of them—
riverbank caribou—the women in the cabin
believe this is the word I want. Maybe I've never
been here
                    as much as
fossil grass in the creek
                              the road eating
hulled ribcage and hefting
                                        these words
so I won't forget. Aren't we red sun
                                        distant

after the funeral? Still we are
crane, now, maybe bear
willows—consuming thick
red muscle.

THE SEAFOOD PLANT

I thought all summer with the heavy ache of machinery,
the sixteen-hour ache. Sore arms, sore back, sprained fingers,
broken arches in my aching feet, and O God
the smell of me when I got home.
I sank into the couch beside my sister, my dad,
and saw them wrinkle up, and all I wanted
was to sit or cuss, to eat or shower, and never
to go to bed. I didn't want to let go
of the book, the line, the letter. I held onto
the television show. If I did not sleep
I would not be called back into worn jeans,
shapeless shirts, and a snot rag for a head handkerchief.
Back into rubber boots, hairnets,
and industrial rubber gloves still damp from the dryer.
Back into the smelly yellow apron that hung heavy on
     my tense neck.
Back into my grim face and taut back, O hell, O damn,
I've got to pay for college.

As I set up the thermometer tests,
core temperature paperwork,
as I watched the temperature drop
in the brine freezer, I heard the sound of overflowing
water and tried to laugh at the season-old joke.
The joke's on me, I always forget and the cooker overflows,
I'm always tired, but I am awake, Rocky.

"Oh yeah, yeah, that's good crab."
Sure. "Maybe too salty?"
I checked the salinity.
"Let's go check it again."
Sure. "Whew! Did you smell the fifth on Pete?"
Yeah, crazy. "These guys, when I worked in the Aleutians—"

~~~

Rocky Piccini, the Italian fishmonger, skilled,
still blue-eyed as he was when he was twenty in Seattle,
and probably still gets as many women,
though not girls. He wanted a case of liquor,
his preferred method of baiting. He called from Unalakleet
    asking
if we wanted salmon eggs for fishing, and we did.

It's a strange place to think about—your soul,
and science, all that biology can muddle up your head,
at least, if your head were my head.

And it did, and I'd walk between the cooker, the chiller,
the brine freezer thermometer in hand,
testing the waters,
taking the temperature,
and recording time.

This second year at it—bored,
the novelty of the new level
of hell had worn off.

I practiced squaring numbers in my head,
until the novelty of that wore off.

I practiced phrases in French,
Je n'aime pas les crabes.
Ils ont beaucoup de jambes.
Je cuise des crabes toujours.

I thought about the mystery of God
who was *partout* but seemed
to have forgotten to write
to my small church. Sheltered,
the questions that went unposed
were now tearing me apart.
Above me were white ceilings gray with flies.

The concrete floor colored with the yellow
guts of crab wrenched out of them
by the orange rubber-gloved hands of Eskimos
who hate our jobs—sometimes a worker
shows up half-shot and I have to send them home,
trembling with timid authority—the last damn job you can get
and I've got to send you home.

THERE IS A CERTAIN SLANT OF LIGHT

in the seafood plant, earplugs
muffling the din of industrial
butchery, the garage door open
on the small boat harbor,
a seagull landing on the damp
pavement, for all their gut
eating, they are beautiful
in the long daylight as I watch,
crab jelly gray on my white
apron, cleaning the yellow crab
shit from my gloves.

IT'S HARD TO WRITE ON A BOX

the weight of four fish
carcasses is ____,
in Sharpie, on the waxed
surface, white flaking off,
no flourishes, hand cramped,
and the weight of another
that other
the thing that happened
that summer
my cousin dying
collapsing in the fish plant office
        this is the last place to be
        and this is the last place
and the feeling
maybe I could have done more
CPR or rescue breathing.

The Pepsi can he held
as he fell, lid partially popped,
phone dangling from its cord.

And after, hands trembling,
wondering if I could ask to hold
a co-worker's hand as they wheeled
him out.

HELICOPTER WEEK AT BLM

I thought bleached
meant dry as I reached
for the knuckle
branch and yanked—the drowned
shrub brown-curl-anchored
to the creek bed bent
and held until the neck-twist crack
severed it and set me off
balance with its release. If
I can remember every
detail, I'll be saved.
The brown algae exploded
in every rocky water
pocket. I stepped
on uneven creek bed, the fish
lay on their sides, eyes
in and poked out—
frog-egg-semen-thick-and-
jellied-cream skin.
I poked him—
the dead male
lying nose to the north,
eye creamed over,
the film didn't give
way easy. I dropped
the stick, got in
the truck, we drove away.

MOOSE HUNT CLOGYRNACH

The bull moose moves down the mountain,
we follow, finding now and then
hoof signs into brush,
fresh scat on the moss.
Willows lush,
skirt the mounds.

Sister and I feign light footfall,
as we follow, Dad, the moose trail,
and the arcing sun.
I'm handed a gun.
It's funny,
appalling,

I have never wanted to shoot:
Likely I'd beat bears with gun butt,
bullets enchambered,
while I remembered,
dismembered,
how to shoot.

A heavy, heaving sound before:
the beast is quaking. Rich brown fur,
one staggering eye
rolling brown then white.
Bloodied hide,
tundra floor.

The moose shudders down with broken knee,
moved, brother raises rifle deftly,
then the hunter's son,
fires his gun
and sits stunned
near the trees.

Through the blood-painted leaves we have come
panting. Dad shoves branches out of
the way, bastinade
parade of faded
leaves falls straight
from willows.

Dad's first to step into the grove
of bushes. In the yellow cove
brother rests, now stands,
gestures with his hands
how the moose moved
to its end.

Over its gleaming hide we bend.
Split thick skin, heavy blood scent
lisps from awkward stronghold
to last unfolding—
the socket,
the brisket.

CATHERINE AT TEN,

this is a poem for you—violets are blue
on the tundra hill. Eyelids pressed, still

red light shines through the thin skin.
Prettiful flowers' stems, how your brown skin blends

into the grass as we hike past
barren blueberry plants and advance on ptarmigan nests.

Roses are red—nothing is said,
I memorize lichen crackle lines,

the green sheen of the stem in my hand,
the curl of your wild hair unfurling.

Remember the ground crunch sound,
the way we look around

and Mom and Dad with the buckets?

ANOTHER KIND OF LOVE POEM

The wind
shook loose the mosquitoes from their
tight bunch into a spray of fanning legs
and tattoo wings,
spreading the fine and buzzing dust
into an ashen sky.

Drawn into sky
those fine things made visible the blank clime. A starry wind,
an eddy spreading trembling dust
into length and height, a distance measured by their
interlocking wings
and spare and splinter legs.

With that sudden sweep—legs
disappearing into heightened sky—
the harsh singing of their wings
swallowed by the wind
suddenly became incalculable. Their
abrupt inanimacy, with uneasy ease their corporeal matter
    transformed to dust.

Uneasily, I reached down to brush the dust
of their crushed legs
and smeared bodies, their
ink-print skin-stains from the red welts on my arms, eyes on
    the sky,
waiting for the small wind
to fail and for the small wings

wavering on the small wind, those small wings
bearing the voracious dust.
The small wind
spreading legs

≈

that land invisible to seeing skin, those small legs invisible in
    the great sky,
those small things and their

small desire hovering over me, their
entire bodies a desire, winging
their desire through the windy sky.
They became dust.
They with their feathered legs
rode high on the wind.

Imagine their scattered, dusty
fall, wings to carry them, legs,
light as sky, to land like wind on the warm body of their desired.

LET THE BUNTINGS BE OUR VALENTINE

The snow bunting rises over the tar paper roof, twig feet nearly scratching the flashing—a bumblebee's burst and tumble—trefoil feet and delicate dark nails flick the green gritted sand, three others follow—their downy breasts (soft lunar eclipses) lead hearts indiscernible, but they must be red and perfect berries buried in thick tundra moss, dense and brown, caged in white lichen claws. How my Aapa loves them—their white breasted surge into the white winter sky, the small of their voices as they speck and disappear.

SESTINA

—for Andrew

In that dark night glimmer, I latch
my bee
wings to your heart's orb. A fin
of shadow climbs the willows.
Deep in the rocks a dark
vein—I will XXXX my love in those gray stones.

In my hands are many stones—
my fingers latch
then loose and trace dark
sea shapes, seaweed being
swayed (a receded sea), this is a willowy
branch, this a willowy leaf, this a fin,

and another fin
caught up in the gray, flaking stones.
Above the ancient carbon willows rock live willows.
Deep dark bark latches
willow spine to spine, B
of my heart, how will the dark

earth cup us—how will our dark
impressions fin
their way into the earth's long future? The best
fossils are stones
of agony, the creature arches, gasping, through all the ages. We latch
onto them, the effort of it all, the brutal end, will we

end, our dark and burning bodies, rocked beneath some thin willows
swaying beneath that still young sun, or will all darken,
unlatch,
fin.
I carry in my heart a small stone,
my darling, you are beautiful,

let all be
transfixed a moment, you stand beside willows
the dark earth tumbles over the smooth river stones.
The river rises. The dark
earth's long-ago finally
surfaces, two creatures latched,

a small bee clings to the dark
willow branch, you find
that stone and my fingers latch around it.

HE TRIMMED THE APPLE TREE.

Another age passed,
this one marked
by a child's bare legs
kicking in the cold air
as he watched his father
standing on the aluminum
ladder, pruning shears
an offering to the sky.

IMIQMUIT, FROM THE WATER,

they arrive
in my dreams
on the water
they ply the waves
in the coastal fog
paddles a soft sucking sound
like their babies on the breast
like my baby on my breast
like breath

they return
my family
my ancestors
it is summer
they are coming to the mainland
where we live now
even in winter
Ugiuvak, but they have that
secret place
we wish we had
all together
even then though
they also came for summer
to this rocky
windswept beach

we are waiting
bated breath
our hearts open
for your images
for your lives
to inspire us
to compel us
into dancing
into fishing
into sharing our food together
in the cabin as the fog rolls quietly by

TIIMIAQ, SOMETHING CARRIED,

—for Joan Naviyuk Kane

in a book
        we read about these things
        in a book
                carved figures
aŋun, aġ naq, migiqłiq

each word I know
as a dictionary
entry
take this away
and give paper
in return

my tongue against the ink
is English
naluaġmiut
sucking in the flimsy fibers
spewing out a stumbling word
I teach them to Sinaġuk and Paniataaq
all wrong
they round the words in their small mouths
small rivers, small stones
don't pity me, they are heavy stones
but they are the small rivers
I drop the stones into

        Classrooms stand between us, Aakaŋ
        but their language classes taught me
        how to learn from books.

        The years I spent away at college
        bring me back, Aakaŋ.
        This is how to learn a foreign tongue
        from books.

~~~

still, from a leather pouch small figures
tumble out—aŋun—perhaps aaŋauraq or iŋmi—his hood
    around his shoulders
aġnak—perhaps nuliaq—how tenderly her brown atigi is
    distinguished

atausiq qituġnaklu atausiq paniklu
one and one
tiimiaq in a small pouch, in a pocket or aġġinaq,
like portraits on my phone
in case of long separation
the ice floe shakes loose and tumbles him south
a village, elsewhere, all winter
they are remembered
just so, tenderly, the small figures,
placeholders, bringing to mind his beloved.
even now the residual tenderness
travels across the sterile page
the image of the images
of the beloved
love refracted through the making cannot be contained
in the dry clinical photo, even now,
the beloved tug patiently across the distant page
at the thread strung between their hearts
even the collection
the price of the sale
of the figures
their storage in a catalogued archive (or disposal)
cannot undo the stringing of that tenderness and memory
it strums a note familiar, but unique,
one reaching towards four
the hands that carved them to remember
and distance that memory traveled
and tugged at his heart, remain.

≈

just so, I carry this memory with me,
of Ugiuvak, of four women and a man climbing
a steep ice cliff

and a small gathering of poets
each of us making, just so, our small figures
to be carried
what we are making cannot be undone

CATHERINE, AT 18

Everything is a reminder of
          YOUR TOTAL RESPONSIBILITY
of
          PLUS, MEMBERS SAVE
          SOULEVER
          LIFT
Formulated especially to
          EACH ACCIDENT
Fortified with
Vitamins and Minerals
          OTHER THAN COLLISION

of here take another breath, here,

          of crows spinning hard
          on axis to hit the hawk again

of each life is this fine thread
spun out
          the curl of the small hope
reaching out to the other
will it touch anything or
nothing of how does the
heart hold fast

          fly hawk
          fly crow

a small white chicken
crossed our yard
strutting her night's
un-housed survival

sometimes in summer
the river's cool contrasts
appreciatively with the air
here the willows burn beside
the road and lunch chars on
green branches
        oh sister.
we are all finding our way,
          breath by breath

here is my hand, as we used to do,
step forward.

ROUGHLY FOR THE NORTH

I am beginning to think I want to live like you,
to take up this dead swan with two brown arms
to carry the swooning body to the chopping block
to lay it down, the elegant arch of its white body
stops my heart.

I prod its heart beneath its feathers, stilled—
the tongue out of the orange beak
is black with things it should have sung.

Vainamoinen sang into existence a boat
to sail North. In seeking this magic he destroyed

a flock of swans. Did they look like this?
Did the long line of their spines arch like this?
I wish I were a dancer to let lines fall like that.
But I am dressed like you, roughly for the North.

Is my hand strong as your blue-veined hand?
So I may take up the red hatchet
to chop off the wing with one strike,
to unbalance the bird, and broken,
do I sing its death song for you?

Holding a white wing in hand,
you stand from your stooping
the line of your back quilted by a blue overcoat.
Do I remember this or is this all conjecture
or conjure? But here you hand the wing to me,

and there, you keep the swan wing at your side.
I am mute with complexities, and I want words, as you
kneeling before the stove sweep away ashes
with the long-pinioned wing.

≈

As you move sand with the bowed span of feathers
into a dustpan you empty
by the chopping block, I realize,
Aaka, I seek a song for you,
so I lift the hatchet and let it fall.

PART THREE

EPILOGUE

AFTERLIFE, III

I hope it's an island with the indigo waters,

beloved, where you are. May your cabin
be lit and warm, hold your children
to your breast (they were too long
away from you), and watch for me. I will
come in a boat loaded with bread
and milk and meat. It will be so full.
We will drink tea. We will watch
the terns and seagulls from the seaward
window. In the summer you will be young,
your body lithe, you will climb
the cliffs to the puffin, murre, and seagull
nests. You will carry their cone-shaped eggs
home in your pockets—hollow them out—
the blue eggs speckled with black—string
them—knot them—hang them
from the rafters—fragile globes—read
my fortune in their marks—what joy,
what sorrow separates me from you.

In winter, if it is in winter, I will set
out by sledge. I will be sure
to bring a seal home for you to dress.

I will be sure at last to catch
my breath when I first see you.